The Little Book of Growing Things

Gardening activities for the Foundation Stage

Written by Sally Featherstone

Illustrations by Sarah Featherstone

LITTLE BOOKS WITH BIG IDEAS

Reprinted 2011
Published 2009 by A&C Black Publishers Limited
36 Soho Square, London W1D 3QY
www.acblack.com

First published by Featherstone Education Ltd, July 2003

ISBN 978-1-9041-8768-4

© Featherstone Education Ltd, 2003
Text © Sally Featherstone, 2003
Illustrations © Sarah Featherstone, 2003
Series Editor, Sally Featherstone
A CIP record for this publication is available from
the British Library.

Printed in Great Britain by Latimer Trend & Company Limited.

This book is produced using paper that is made from wood grown
inmanaged, sustainable forests. It is natural, renewable and
recyclable.

The logging and manufacturing processes conform to the
environmental regulations of the country of origin.

**To see our full range of titles
visit www.acblack.com**

Contents

Introduction

The Little Book of Growing Things has been written to help you to organise and present what can be some of the most enjoyable activities in your setting. You don't need a lot of space, time or money to make sure the children you work with experience nature, both indoors and outside.

Being outside, enjoying nature, digging, watching flowers and insects, watering, collecting, examining and using their senses are all lasting childhood experiences. Children spend less time outside than ever before, so we must give them these vital experiences in our settings if we want them to have wonderful memories of planting, growing, watching and even eating plants themselves. How else will they know where tomatoes, apples, lettuce or strawberries come from and how they grow?

Gardening is also a wonderful way of making friends and contacts in your community – elderly people, neighbours, parents and shopkeepers can all be involved in your projects, and can enhance them with their own contributions of knowledge, experience, plant material, seeds and even help in your garden. Many parents and friends who might not otherwise feel comfortable helping may be only too willing to become involved in making a garden, planting bulbs, watering vegetables, contributing cuttings, building paths, seats and walls.

Local shops and stores may also be willing to help. Garden centres and DIY stores will often donate things. If gardening stores are going to prosper, they will need gardeners, not couch potatoes, in the future!

And gardening does not all have to happen outdoors in the summer! Indoor gardens and gardening, planting bulbs and seeds, making compost and planting trees can all happen in the winter too. Digging is a good way to keep children (and adults) warm on cold or damp days, and indoor plants need care all the year round.

Safety, health and hygiene

We are all responsible for the health and well being of the children in our care. However, that doesn't mean we should be so over careful that children never have the opportunity to work with plants and the soil!

Reasonable care must of course be taken when children are working with tools and with seeds and compost. However, if sensible precautions are taken, children can have all the benefits that come from growing flowers, vegetables and fruits, while remaining safe.

Some simple precautions

▶ Make sure there is always an adult present when children are gardening.

▶ Teach children to always wash their hands after gardening, and not to put dirty fingers in their mouths.

▶ Some seeds, leaves and flowers are harmful to children if eaten or touched. Always check that the seeds and plants you use are safe for your garden.

▶ Teach children that they must never eat berries, leaves or flowers without checking with an adult that they are safe. This is particularly important on seed or plant collecting walks.

▶ Buy some simple plant books that tell you which plants are safe.

▶ Check for allergies to pollen, plants or other substances. Provide gloves for allergic children, and any others who may find handing soil distasteful at first.

▶ Choose and store tools carefully. Hooks, baskets, boxes, trays and hanging pockets are all useful for safety and tidiness.

▶ If children are digging directly in the soil, check for debris such as glass, animal droppings and other hazards.

▶ Never use chemicals when gardening with young children.

▶ Cover any cuts or broken skin.

▶ You may need to use scissors or knives. Take particular care to ensure that children do not have access to anything sharp.

Independence

Once children have been introduced to the activity, the tools and the rules, gardening should ideally be an independent activity as well as an adult directed one. Of course you will be planning some activities to link with specific projects, topics and times of the year, but there should also be times when gardening is a child initiated activity, full of play, practice and fun.

Children should have regular opportunities to dig, shift, pour, water, pile, lift, shovel, rake, fill, plant and weed, alongside such activities as riding bikes, climbing, jumping and running.

...and what are they learning?

Here are some of the Early Learning Goals associated with gardening and growing things indoors and out:

In Personal, Social and Emotional Development
- to continue to be interested, excited and motivated to learn
- to be confident to try new activities

In Communication, Language and Literacy
- to interact with others, negotiating plans and activities
- to extend their vocabulary, exploring the meanings and sounds of new words
- to use talk to organise, sequence and clarify thinking, ideas, feelings and events
- to attempt writing for various purposes

Problem Solving, Reasoning and Numeracy
- to use language such as 'greater', 'smaller', 'heavier' or 'lighter' to compare quantities
- to use everyday words to describe position
- to use developing mathematical ideas and methods to solve practical problems

In Knowledge and Understanding of the World
- to investigate objects and materials by using all of their senses as appropriate
- to find out about, and identify, some features of living things and events they observe
- to look closely at similarities, differences, patterns and change
- to ask questions about why things happen and how things work
- to observe, find out about and identify features in the place they live and the natural world
- to find out about their environment and talk about those features they like and dislike

In Physical Development
- to move with control and co-ordination
- to recognise the importance of keeping healthy and those things which contribute to this
- to use a range of small and large equipment
- to handle tools, objects and materials safely and with increasing control

In Creative Development
- to explore colour, texture, shape, form and space in two and three dimensions
- to respond in a variety of ways to what they see, hear, smell, touch and feel

Get Digging!

Children love digging and they need plenty of experience of handling, moving, exploring and digging before they can take on the responsibility of plants and gardening!

What they are learning by digging:

In Personal, Social and Emotional Development
to continue to be interested and motivated to learn
to be confident to try new activities

In Communication
to interact with others

Problem Solving, Reasoning and Numeracy
to use language to compare quantities
to use everyday words to describe position

In Knowledge and Understanding of the World
to investigate objects and materials by using all of their senses as appropriate
to find out about their environment, and talk about those features they like and dislike

In Physical Development
to move with control and co-ordination to use a range of small and large equipment;
to handle tools, objects and materials safely

In Creative Development
to respond in a variety of ways to what they see, hear, smell, touch and feel

What you need

▶ a wheelbarrow, sand or water tray, builder's tray (also known as a Tough Spot), or big bowl

▶ spades, spoons, scoops, rakes, trowels and other tools

▶ soil or compost (with or without gravel, grass, stones, real worms etc.) this activity is best done with real soil dug from a garden, but a grow bag is a good substitute if you really can't get the real stuff

▶ plastic worms, spiders etc. can make this activity very inviting!

Health and Safety
Don't use soil from areas where animals or pets have been, and make sure children wash their hands thoroughly after they have played with any natural materials.

What you do

1. Tip the soil/compost in the container.
   Protect children's clothing with aprons or old shirts.
2. Join the children as they explore, dig, handle and investigate the soil or compost. Listen to what they are saying as they work.
3. Work alongside them, talking about what you are doing, how the soil feels, looks and smells.
4. Add some magnifying glasses or bug pots.

Some alternative digging experiences

If you have a place where children can dig directly into the ground, this is even better. Here they can really explore digging, moving, lifting and replacing the soil. Provide some wheelbarrows, trucks or trolleys so they can move the soil from place to place. Leave an area of your garden for this activity, if you possibly can. Remember that some children love digging, but have no interest in gardening or growing plants.

The benefits of digging

Digging strengthens wrists, hands, fingers and arms. It develops the muscles needed for drawing, writing, making, exploring and using tools. Talking about digging develops language and thinking. Moving things develops collaboration as well as language and physical dexterity. Exploration is a scientific skill.

Flower Pots

Flowers can be grown in any sort of container, but you don't have to buy them. Many familiar objects can be used to make decorative, amusing or unusual containers for indoors or out.

What they are learning by making flower pots:

In Personal, Social and Emotional Development
to continue to be interested and motivated
to learn to be confident to try new activities

In Communication, Language and Literacy
to extend their vocabulary, exploring the meanings and sounds of new words

Problem Solving, Reasoning and Numeracy
to use language such as 'greater', 'smaller', 'heavier' or 'lighter' to compare quantities

In Knowledge and Understanding of the World
to investigate objects and materials by using all of their senses as appropriate

In Physical Development
to use a range of small and large equipment
to handle tools, objects and materials safely

In Creative Development
to explore colour, texture, shape, form and space in two and three dimensions

Old tyres

Fill the centre of an old tyre (or pile up two or three tyres) and plant with annuals, shrubs or vegetables.

Or get someone to help you turn a tyre inside out to make a patio planter.

Put chunks of polystyrene in the bottom of big containers – it makes the pot lighter and saves on compost.

Pots and pans

Cups, jugs, bowls, mugs – any old, cracked or chipped crockery (but nothing too sharp) from the kitchen can become containers. Put a layer of gravel in the bottom, or stand a plastic pot inside, so the soil can drain. Children love making miniature gardens in soup plates, small trays and saucers.

Decorate!

Decorate plain plant pots with shells, beads, buttons, glitter etc. Cover the pot with a layer of DIY filler, then press the decorations in. Seal with a coat of varnish or PVA glue when dry.

Sponge printing, rubber stamps and stencils can also be used effectively.

Or use old seed catalogues to make a collage and seal it with dilute PVA glue or varnish. These pots last better if you keep them indoors.

Have some fun!

Try planting flowers in one of these unusual containers:

▶ a pair of trainers

▶ a pair of wellies

▶ a watering can

▶ a baby's potty

▶ a fireman's helmet

▶ a colander

▶ an old bird cage.

Hang it

Plant up old baskets or buckets and hang them from trees or door frames. If you buy summer basket plants after Easter, they are much cheaper! Or plant pansies, herbs or heather for a winter basket.

Make sure the baskets are very secure and checked frequently – a basket full of wet compost and plants is heavy!

...and the cheap option!

Recycle old plastic plant pots (make sure they have been washed first). Or you could use yogurt pots, margarine tubs, plastic cups or cut-off drinks bottles. Bottles with handles make portable planters. Make some holes in the bottom of all these for drainage.

Vegetable and Fruit Gardens

You don't need a plot of soil to make a vegetable or fruit garden, but vegetables do need more room for their roots and more water, so they need deeper containers.

What they are learning by growing fruit and vegetables:

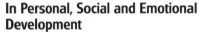

In Personal, Social and Emotional Development
to continue to be interested, and motivated
to learn to be confident to try new activities

In Communication, Language and Literacy
to interact with others, negotiating plans

In Knowledge and Understanding of the World
to investigate objects and materials by using all of their senses as appropriate
to find out about, and identify, some features of living things and events they observe
to ask questions about why things happen
to observe features in the natural world

In Physical Development
to recognise the importance of keeping healthy and those things which contribute to this

In Creative Development
to respond in a variety of ways to what they see, hear, smell, touch, taste and feel

Grow bags

Grow bags are an ideal, cheap place to grow vegetables – beans, lettuce, tomatoes, herbs, peppers and courgettes. Put the bag against a wall and use strings or canes for the plants to climb up.

Why not try a plant mixture and add some sweet peas or nasturtiums? You could also add some herbs or lettuces for flavour.

Strawberries

Strawberries are very easy to grow and children love them!

Strawberry pots have little pockets in them, so the plants get plenty of sun. Look for a terracotta or plastic one at a garden centre. Or make your own by propping up a grow bag and cutting pockets in the plastic for the plants. Keep the bag on a slope in the sun.

More berries!

Blackberries, loganberries, tayberries and blueberries can all be grown in containers. Make sure you choose thorn-free varieties of blackberries and tayberries. A gooseberry bush in a big container will be a discussion point. The only problem is – all gooseberries have prickles!

Roll out the barrel

Plastic or wooden barrels (cut in half) make great vegetable or flower gardens. They are stable, hold a good amount of soil, and are raised so children can get at them easily to watch, smell and feel the plants growing. Try planting carrots, potatoes or sweetcorn in your barrel (see page 58).

Fruit trees

A standard or dwarf variety of fruit tree will grow well in a tub, barrel or planter. Make sure you water it well (every day) and you should be able to enjoy home-grown fruit. Plums, apples, cherries, peaches and nectarines all come in dwarf and container varieties. Always check that the tree is grafted on a dwarf or M27 rootstock.

...and the cheap option!

Use black plastic rubbish sacks to make your own grow bags. Put one bag inside the other (for strength) and fill with recycled or DIY compost (see page 52).

A home-made bag is a good place to grow potatoes, lettuce, tomatoes or other salad crops: they even work on window-sills.

Quick Growers (flowers)

Quick results are important when gardening with children, whether this is a bean in a jam jar or a sunflower competition. Here are some ideas for quick growing plants with flowers.

What they are learning by growing their own flowers:

In Personal, Social and Emotional Development
to be confident to try new activities

In Communication, Language and Literacy
to use talk to organise and sequence events

Problem Solving, Reasoning and Numeracy
to use everyday words to describe position

In Knowledge and Understanding of the World
to find out about, and identify, some features of living things and events they observe
to look closely at change to observe the natural world

In Physical Development
to handle tools, objects and materials safely and with increasing control

In Creative Development
to explore colour, texture, shape, form and space in two and three dimensions
to respond in a variety of ways to what they see, hear, smell, touch and feel

Some quick growing varieties

Climbers
▶ Mile Minute Vine, Morning Glory, Sweet Peas, Passion Flower, Nasturtium, Clematis Montana, Honeysuckle

Annuals (these can also be grown indoors on a sunny window-sill)
▶ Marigolds, Love in a Mist, Poppies, Daisies, Sunflowers

Biennials (these grow leaves the first year and flower in the second)
▶ Foxgloves and Wallflowers are biennials.

Wild flowers (these really need to be outdoors with some space)
▶ All wild flowers grow quickly to make the most of summer! Remember, it is against the law to pick flowers in the wild, but you can collect their seeds.

What you do

1. Climbers all like having their roots in a cool place, so plant them with their feet in the shade. They all need support – if you haven't got a wall, try a tepee of canes, a trellis (in or out of a container), or some strings attached to a broom handle hammered into the ground.

2. If you buy a packet of children's seeds – they are usually annuals and sold as a variety – you will have plenty for several big tubs or a large border. Sow these annuals direct into freshly dug and raked soil and cover them with a very thin layer of soil. Water them with a fine sprinkler or watering can.

3. Wild flower seeds can be sown in the same way. Either buy a packet or two, or collect some seeds this year on walks and country visits, and sow them next year. Don't forget to label the seed envelopes and keep them somewhere dry.

Remember
▶ some ready-forced bulbs during the winter
▶ some pansies or polyanthus in the early spring
▶ an amaryllis for a real show and a fascinating growth rate!

...and the cheap option!
Keep an eye on your local garden centre for out of date seeds and bargain plants. They may even give them to your setting.

Quick Growers (to eat)

Some vegetables and fruit are quick to grow and are soon ready to eat. How about picking your own salad or snipping some mustard and cress for a snack sandwich?

What they are learning by growing their own food:

In Personal, Social and Emotional Development
to be confident to try new activities

In Communication, Language and Literacy
to extend their vocabulary, exploring the meanings and sounds of new words

In Knowledge and Understanding of the World
to investigate objects and materials by using all of their senses as appropriate

to find out about, and identify, some features of living things
to observe, find out about and identify features in the place they live and the natural world

In Physical Development
to recognise the importance of keeping healthy and those things which contribute to this

In Creative Development
to respond in a variety of ways to what they see, hear, smell, touch and feel

Ideas for indoors

1. Grow some salad bowl lettuce in a window box – you can pull leaves from this variety without cutting the whole plant, which goes on to grow more leaves for another time!

2. Buy a packet of mustard and cress seeds. Cut up an old (clean) towel and use it to line some (clean) plastic food trays. Water the trays and sprinkle on the seeds. Keep them damp. The children will be able to watch them grow over a few days until they are ready to cut and eat in egg sandwiches.

3. Tell the story of 'Jack and the Beanstalk' and plant some beans. You could plant one for each child in a plastic cup so they can watch their own bean grow (have a few in reserve in case there are failures!). You could grow some in jars lined with paper towels. Trap the beans between the paper and the glass, put a small amount of water in the jar and watch the roots go down and the shoots go up.

4. Draw a face on half an egg shell, add a little soil and sprinkle with grass seed, alfalfa or cress. Watch the grass grow into green hair!

Ideas for outdoors

1. Plant flowers or vegetables in a grow bag or in the soil. Watch for the shoots to emerge, then give them sticks or strings to grow up. Watch how they attach themselves to the strings – look for the tiny spirals of tendrils feeling for the supports. Measure their growth every day. Good vegetable plants to grow this way are beans, peas and courgettes, and you could add sweet peas to make a perfumed garden.

2. If you have a bigger plot, some tubs or more grow bags, you could plant some more fast growers. Try carrots, radishes, lettuce, chives, spinach, sugar peas or spring onions. These are not as quick as mustard or beans, but they will be ready in a few weeks, rather than months!

3. Some more exotic quick growers are lamb's lettuce and rocket.

4. Rhubarb grows quickly, and a rhubarb plant will come up every year to feed you again. Be careful: rhubarb leaves are poisonous if eaten in quantity!

5. Sweetcorn will grow into a regular forest if you have room for it. Plant the seeds in small pots on a window-sill and plant out when they are about 5" tall. If you plant them in a circle or a pattern, you can make your own Maize Maze.

...and the cheap option!
Ask parents to donate extra seeds, seedlings and cuttings.

Seeds, Pips and Nuts

Many things we eat have pips, seeds or nuts and some of these will grow into new plants, although they will be unlikely to have fruit that you can eat. Cooked seeds won't grow!

What they are learning by growing seeds, pips and nuts:

In Personal, Social and Emotional Development
to be confident to try new activities

In Communication, Language and Literacy
to extend their vocabulary, exploring the meanings and sounds of new words

Problem Solving, Reasoning and Numeracy
to use everyday words to describe position

In Knowledge and Understanding of the World
to investigate objects and materials
to investigate objects and materials by using all of their senses as appropriate;
to find out about, and identify, some features of living things
to look closely at change
to ask questions about why things happen
to observe, find out about and identify features in the natural world

In Creative Development
to respond in a variety of ways to what they see, hear, smell, touch and feel

What you need

▶ collect some seeds, pips and stones from the fruit and vegetables you eat. Here are some ideas:
Pips from apples, oranges, lemons and grapefruits
Seeds from melons, pumpkins, squash, gourds and marrows
Stones from avocados.

▶ plant pots and potting compost

▶ small plastic bags, lolly sticks and elastic bands

▶ labels cut from a margarine tub and permanent markers

▶ for an avocado stone, you need a jar with a narrow neck, and some toothpicks

What you do

Always wash the seeds and leave them to dry on a paper towel.
Remember, some of the seeds won't grow, so plant plenty!
Some fruit has been treated to keep it fresh during travel and this sometimes sterilises the seeds. You are more likely to be successful if you can get organic produce. If you are not successful the first time, try again.

Apple, orange, lemon, grapefruit etc.

Plant one or two pips in each pot of compost. Put four lolly sticks in the soil round the edge of each pot. Water. Now carefully put a plastic bag over the sticks and fasten with an elastic band round the pot to make a mini greenhouse. Put in a warm, light place and remove the bag when the plant has four leaves. Citrus plants will grow glossy green leaves and perfumed white flowers. Marrows, melons etc. will need to be re-planted outside.

Avocado

Carefully stick four toothpicks (or sharpened matchsticks) into the avocado stone – round the middle, with the pointed end up. Fill the jar with water and rest the avocado stone on the rim of the jar, so the bottom of the stone is in the water. Top up the water when it goes down to keep the bottom of the stone wet.

...and the cheap option!

Grow an indoor potato plant! Follow the instructions for growing a sweet potato vine on page 25.

Seeds for Nothing

Some seeds cost absolutely nothing – except your time in collecting them! Go and look. Seeds are everywhere: in the park, in gardens, in fields, woods, on pavements, in yards, everywhere!

What they are learning by collecting and growing their own seeds:

In Personal, Social and Emotional Development
to be confident to try new activities

In Communication, Language and Literacy
to negotiate plans and activities
to extend their vocabulary
to use talk to sequence events to attempt writing for various purposes

In Knowledge and Understanding of the World
to look closely at similarities, differences, patterns and change

to observe, find out about and identify features in the place they live and the natural world

In Physical Development
to move with control and co-ordination
to use a range of small and large equipment

In Creative Development
to explore colour, texture, shape, form and space in two and three dimensions

What you need

▶ sharp eyes

▶ paper or plastic bags

▶ envelopes

▶ time

Every time you go out, take a bag and keep your eyes open! When you are alone or walking with the children, and especially during late summer and autumn, look for seeds. Here are some you might find:

Tree seeds, such as acorns, conkers and sycamore 'helicopters' (avoid laburnum and yew as they are poisonous); berries from bushes such as hawthorn, sloes and elderberries; seeds from between the scales of fir cones; nuts from hazel or sweet chestnut trees.

Flower seeds in people's gardens, in parks etc. If you ask, people are usually very happy for you to collect seeds from plants in gardens. Some interesting ones are: poppies, delphiniums, foxgloves, ornamental grasses, berries from shrubs and trees such as cotoneaster, holly, berberis and iris.

Weed and wild flower seeds such as dandelion, dock, wild poppy, wild rose hips, blackberries and grass seeds.

What you do

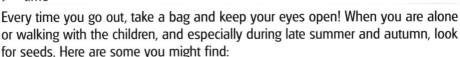

1. Collect the seeds in separate bags and when you get back, put each kind in an envelope or paper bag with the name of the plant and the date you collected the seeds.

2. Many seeds can be planted straight away. Plant big tree seeds in pots (one or two to each pot). Cover them well, water, and put them in a cool, sheltered place outside over the winter. By spring the seeds may have sprouted (if you are lucky!).

3. Put a sprinkling of berries on the surface of some soil in a pot, cover with a thin layer of sand, water and put in a cool, sheltered place outside. Wait until spring to see what has happened.
   N.B. If you put a board or a slate over the pots, it will stop birds and mice from eating your seeds! Don't forget to put a label on each pot to tell you what is growing there.

4. In the spring, scatter your other seeds in pots or in the garden and see what comes up. Every plant that grows is a free one, and every plant that flowers will make more seeds!

Get Sprouting!

Growing seed sprouts to eat in sandwiches and salads is a very satisfying and quick way of gardening. These are usually grown indoors, so you can do this activity all the year round.

What they are learning by growing and eating vegetable sprouts:

In Personal, Social and Emotional Development
to be confident to try new activities

In Communication, language and Literacy
to extend their vocabulary, exploring the meanings and sounds of new words
to use talk to organise, sequence and clarify thinking, ideas, feelings and events

In Knowledge and Understanding of the World
to investigate objects and materials

by using all of their senses as appropriate
to observe, find out about and identify features in the place they live and the natural world

In Physical Development
to recognise the importance of keeping healthy and those things which contribute to this

In Creative Development
to respond in a variety of ways to what they eat

What you need (to grow sprouts in a jar)

▶ mung beans (for bean sprouts), alfalfa seeds or cress seeds

▶ empty jam jars or cut-off plastic bottles

▶ thin fabric (such as net curtain or muslin)

▶ elastic bands

▶ a shallow tray

▶ a dark place or a black rubbish bag

What you do

1. Put a single layer of beans or seeds in the bottom of each jar.

2. Cover with water and leave the seeds to soak over night.

3. The next day, rinse the seeds with clean water and drain.

4. Cover each jar with a piece of fabric and secure it with an elastic band.

5. Tip the jar upside down on the tray so all the water drains out.

6. Put the tray of upside down jars in a dark place (or cover them with a black plastic bag).

7. **Every day**, remove the covers from the jars and rinse the seeds in clean, cold water. Look at them to see how they are growing. Then put the tray of upside down jars back in the dark. Talk about the roots and the shoots. Take a few seeds out of one jar and look at them carefully. Use a magnifying glass to look closely each day. Think about making a daily picture, photo or graph record or diary of your shoots.

8. After a few days the sprouts will be ready to eat.

9. Wash the sprouts and use them in sandwiches or to make a salad.

Make sure you remove any seeds that have not sprouted before you eat them – un-sprouted alfalfa seeds are very hard and particularly painful if eaten by mistake.

Healthy eating note:

Vegetable sprouts are a rich source of vitamin C. Children are always keen to eat anything they have grown themselves, so keep on growing and eating different sorts of sprouts.

Tops and Tails!

Growing plants from the tops and bits of things from the kitchen is good fun and sometimes a big surprise. Here are some to try.

What they are learning by growing tops and tails:

In Personal, Social and Emotional Development
to be confident to try new activities

In Communication, Language and Literacy
to use talk to organise, sequence and clarify events

Problem Solving, Reasoning and Numeracy
to use everyday words to describe position
to use developing mathematical ideas and methods to solve practical problems

In Knowledge and Understanding of the World
to find out about, and identify, some features of living things
to look closely at similarities, differences, patterns and change

In Physical Development
to handle tools, objects, and materials safely and with increasing control

What you need

Tops of vegetables such as:
- ▶ carrot tops (organic carrots grow better!)
- ▶ shallow saucers
- ▶ gravel or small pebbles and water

And for a surprise kitchen plant:
- ▶ sweet potato (you can get one from a supermarket or street market)
- ▶ a glass or plastic jar and some toothpicks
- ▶ a plant pot and some soil or compost

> If you want to be sure of success, buy organically grown sweet potatoes which haven't been sprayed to stop them sprouting in the shops.

What you do (carrot tops)

1. Put some stones or gravel in the saucers.
2. Add water until the stones are just covered.
3. Stand the carrot tops on the stones.
4. Check the water every day.
5. In a few days you will see little bumps on the carrot tops and these will gradually grow into feathery carrot leaves.

What you do (sweet potato vines)

1. You could plant several of these in case one doesn't grow! As with carrots, organic sweet potatoes grow best.
2. Stick a toothpick in each side of each potato, about half way along its length.
3. Fill the jar(s) almost full with lukewarm water.
4. Use the sticks to suspend each potato (pointy end down) over a jar, with its end just in the water.
5. Little roots should appear within 7 – 14 days; tiny sprouts should follow in another week or two (be patient!).
6. Don't forget to check every day and top up the water if necessary.
7. Once the potato has started to grow, it will grow very fast, with ivy-like leaves on long tendrils.
8. When the tendrils are about 15 – 20cm (6 to 8ins) long transplant the vine into a plant pot of soil or compost. You could put it in a hanging basket or a pot on the window-sill so it can trail its leaves and tendrils down.

Don't forget to water regularly.

Plants for Free

Your garden, tub or window box can become a riot of colour and scent without costing you anything except a little compost and some water. Cuttings, runners, leaves and shoots are all free if you know where to look and who to ask.

What they are learning by growing plants for free:

In Communication, Language and Literacy
to use talk to organise, sequence and clarify thinking, ideas, feelings and events

Problem Solving, Reasoning and Numeracy
to use language such as 'greater', 'smaller', 'heavier' or 'lighter' to compare quantities
to use everyday words to describe position

In Knowledge and Understanding of the World
to find out about, and identify, some features of living things, objects and events they observe
to look closely at similarities, differences, patterns and change
to ask questions about why things happen and how things work
to observe, find out about and identify features in the place they live and the natural world

In Creative Development
to respond in a variety of ways to what they see, hear, smell, touch and feel

Getting plants for free ——————————

1. Cuttings

Many plants will grow from cuttings. Tradescantia, ivy and busy Lizzie cuttings will even root in a glass of water! Most house plants are easy to propagate by taking cuttings in early summer.

▶ Cut small lengths (2 – 4ins/5 – 10cm) of non-flowering shoots from new growth which is soft and green.

▶ Remove the leaves from the bottom half of each cutting and stick them in small pots of compost, about three cuttings to each.

▶ Water, cover with a plastic bag and elastic band, or the bottom of a plastic bottle.

▶ Leave in a light place, away from direct sun, until new growth appears, then remove the cover and put each new plant in a pot of its own.

2. Runners

Some plants send out runners (roots with little plants on the end). Common ones are strawberries and spider plants.

▶ Put a small pot of soil next to the parent plant.

▶ Carefully put the little plantlet on the soil and peg down the root with a stone, a hair pin, a paper clip or a small 'U' shaped piece of wire.

▶ Make sure the soil is crumbly and keep it damp.

▶ When the plantlet has rooted in its new pot, cut the joining root.

▶ The little runners will soon grow into bigger plants, which then produce runners of their own.

3. Leaf cuttings

Some plants will grow from their own leaves! African violets, gloxinias and begonias are good plants to start with.

▶ Cut one or two healthy leaves from a strong parent plant.

▶ Make holes in the soil in small pots with a pencil, and push the leaves in until the stalk is buried and the leaf rests on the edge of the pot.

▶ The leaf will produce little roots and a small plant will grow at the place where the leaf joins the soil.

Wild, Weed and Pavement

There are more free plants in gardens, paths and waste ground. These are usually described as weeds, but a weed is only 'a plant in the wrong place.' Always ask the owner if you are collecting plants from their land, even if it looks wild!

What they are learning by growing wild plants and weeds:

In Personal, Social and Emotional Development
to be confident to try new activities

Problem Solving, Reasoning and Numeracy
to use everyday words to describe position

In Knowledge and Understanding of the World
to investigate objects and materials by using all of their senses as appropriate
to find out about, and identify, some features of living things they observe

to observe, find out about and identify features in the place they live and the natural world
to find out about their environment, and talk about those features they like and dislike

In Creative Development
to explore colour, texture, shape, form and space in two and three dimensions
to respond in a variety of ways to what they see, hear, smell, touch and feel

Some wild and weedy plants to try:

- daisies
- wild hops
- buttercups
- dandelions
- celandines
- clover
- thistles
- cow parsley

- bindweed
- buddleia
- speedwell
- dead nettle
- golden rod
- ragwort
- willow herb

What you do

1. Take a plastic bag and a small trowel as you go for a walk.
2. You could photograph or make a note of the plants in their natural surroundings (shady, sunny, wet, muddy, in grass etc.), so you can make sure they are happy in their new homes.
3. Make sure you dig the roots up as well as the plant, and group the plants you find together in separate bags.
4. When you get the plants back to your setting, replant them in pots, tubs or grow bags. Try to keep plants with their friends, and put them in their favourite position.
5. Water the plants each day.
6. Remember that many of the plants you find this way are annuals – they only live for one season. When they have flowered, collect your own seeds from them, label carefully and keep them to sow next year.

If you don't know the names of weeds and wild plants, get a copy of:

The Wildlife Trust Guide to Wild Flowers – ISBN 9 781843 421.

It has all the common wild flowers with their common names and where they grow – and the royalties go to the Wild flower Trust Charity. If you contact your local Wildlife Trust, they will give you further information on wild flowers and other wildlife issues.

House Plants

If you haven't got access to a garden outside, make a garden indoors. You can use tubs, pots, window boxes, planters, trays and many other sorts of containers, including hanging baskets, filled with indoor plants and flowers.

What they are learning by growing plants indoors:

In Personal, Social and Emotional Development
to be confident to try new activities

In Communication, Language and Literacy
to use talk to organise, sequence and clarify thinking, ideas, feelings and events

Problem Solving, Reasoning and Numeracy
to use everyday words to describe position

In Knowledge and Understanding of the World
to observe, find out about and identify features in the place they live and the natural world
to find out about their environment, and talk about those features they like and dislike

In Physical Development
to handle tools, objects, and materials safely and with increasing control

In Creative Development
to respond in a variety of ways to what they see, hear, smell, touch and feel

Some ideas for easy plants to grow indoors

Trailing or hanging plants

- ▶ spider plant
- ▶ mother of thousands
- ▶ campanula
- ▶ inch plant (tradescantia)

Tall, grassy and foliage plants (some with coloured leaves)

- ▶ umbrella plant
- ▶ ferns
- ▶ baby's tears

Plants with flowers

- ▶ busy Lizzie
- ▶ geranium
- ▶ African violets
- ▶ begonia
- ▶ shrimp plant
- ▶ chrysanthemums

Plants with leaves that smell

- ▶ eucalyptus
- ▶ scented geranium
- ▶ herbs

Long living, hardy plants

- ▶ jade plant
- ▶ geranium
- ▶ African violets
- ▶ most sorts of succulents and all sorts of bulbs

Why not...?

- ▶ Sow some garden annuals, or buy some summer bedding plants (marigolds, lobelia, nasturtium, morning glory, petunia etc.) and grow these indoors. As long as they have plenty of light and water, they will grow and flower.

- ▶ Make a garden in an old water tray or even a wheelbarrow. Or make a platform on wheels or castors. Put a plastic tub or container on it. Plant your container with indoor or garden plants and wheel it outside when you go out. If you put big chunks of polystyrene in the bottom, under the compost, it will be lighter and easier to move.

- ▶ Plant some hanging baskets with summer basket plants and hang them in the windows of your setting or from a hook in the top of the door frame, where the plants can get plenty of light.

- ▶ Use indoor creepers or climbers to make living green screens and dividers inside your setting.

- ▶ Ask parents and friends for donations of house plants that have outgrown their welcome or their pots, or for cuttings and baby plantlets.

More Fruity Business

If you grow fruit in your garden, you will attract interest from birds, insects, animals and even humans, but growing fruit is a great learning experience and it tastes wonderful!

What they are learning by growing fruit in the garden:

In Personal, Social and Emotional Development
to continue to be interested, excited and motivated to learn and to be confident to try new activities

In Communication, Language and Literacy
to interact with others, negotiating plans

In Knowledge and Understanding of the World
to investigate objects and materials by using all of their senses as appropriate
to find out about, and identify, some features of living things and events they observe
to ask questions about why things happen
to observe features in the natural world

In Physical Development
to recognise the importance of keeping healthy and those things which contribute to this

In Creative Development
to respond in a variety of ways to what they see, hear, smell, touch and feel

Some fruits to consider

► apples
► strawberries
► blueberries
► blackberries (choose a thornless variety)
► melons
► pumpkins

What you do

► **Apples** – get advice on the best variety for your setting and your area. Many apple trees can now be grown and crop well in containers or small spaces. Apples grafted on M27 rootstock will grow to just 1.5m (5ft.) after ten years. To get a good crop try to find space for two trees, so they can pollinate each other.

► **Strawberries** – choose alpine strawberries to grow in a strawberry pot, or get some small plants and grow them in grow bags, tubs or in the ground. Make sure you choose a disease-resistant variety. Most strawberries will grow and crop every year for three years before you need new plants.

► **Blueberries** – these come from America and are becoming more popular. You will have to wait for a couple of seasons for a heavy crop, but blueberries are disease-resistant, and a plant will last for at least 30 years if you look after it and give it a dressing of leaf mould (decayed fallen leaves) or leafy compost every year.

► **Blackberries** – these are hardy, disease and frost-resistant, and they will grow in almost any soil. Choose a thornless variety so the children can help you to pick them (see index on page 58), a not too vigorous grower, and an early cropper. Make sure you water the plants daily as the fruit begins to change colour from red to black. Then you will get a good crop with lovely juicy berries!

► **Melons** – are good to grow if you have a warm, sunny garden, a conservatory or a big tub. Buy a packet of seeds and try a couple of melon plants. They are annuals, so you will have to plant new seeds every year.

Smell, Feel and Hear a Plant

Gardens are sensory places – make sure yours has things to touch, hear, smell and taste as well as interesting things to see.

What they are learning in a sensory garden:

In Personal, Social and Emotional Development
to continue to be interested, excited and motivated to learn

In Communication, Language and Literacy
to extend their vocabulary, exploring the meanings and sounds of new words

In Knowledge and Understanding of the World
to investigate objects and materials

by using all of their senses as appropriate
to find out about their environment, and talk about those features they like and dislike

In Creative Development
to respond in a variety of ways to what they see, hear, smell, touch and feel

Some suggestions for plants for a sensory garden:

Touchy feely

▶ Furry lamb's ears (Stachys).

▶ Smooth succulents, spiky thistles and hairy grass seeds.

Listen!

▶ Grow grasses and other plants with leaves or seeds that rustle (e.g. sweetcorn and bamboo); flowers with rattly seed pods (e.g. love-in-a-mist); and everlasting flowers with crunchy petals.

▶ Hang things in branches and bushes (CDs, bells and foil dishes).

▶ Put trees and plants where their branches and leaves will tap on windows or hollow containers.

Look at that!

▶ Highly-coloured flowers such as pansies, petunias and sweet peas.

▶ Contrasting colours such as orange and purple or red and white.

▶ Contrasting textures and shapes – grasses next to big leaves and plants with smooth and serrated edges together.

▶ Plants that move in interesting ways e.g. quaking grass.

▶ Plants that have dramatic seed heads or leaves that colour in spring or autumn.

▶ Plants with interesting flowers, such as California or oriental poppies, fuchsia, morning glories, clematis and passion flower.

▶ Shrubs that have coloured stems, catkins or flowers in spring.

Lovely smells!

▶ Lavenders of all sorts – cotton lavender (not a real lavender) has a strong smell, white leaves and yellow daisy flowers.

▶ There are many different sorts of mint, so grow more than one.

▶ Sage, thyme, lemon balm, rosemary, basil and other herbs.

▶ Sweet peas have a lovely, delicate scent.

▶ Chocolate cosmos, which really does smell of chocolate.

▶ Citrus plants have scented oil in their leaves and their flowers smell wonderful!

▶ The curry plant is just what it says – a plant that smells of curry!

Taste it!

▶ Grow your own vegetables, fruit and flowers to eat! (see page 58 for more information on child-friendly varieties).

Butterflies and Bees

Attracting insects is a vital part of gardening. Butterflies, bees, ladybirds, hover flies and dragonflies are all an added interest to children and bring added benefits to your garden.

What they are learning by watching wildlife in the garden:

In Personal, Social and Emotional Development
to continue to be interested, excited and motivated to learn

In Communication, Language and Literacy
to extend their vocabulary

Problem Solving, Reasoning and Numeracy
to extend their vocabulary

In Knowledge and Understanding of the World
to investigate objects and materials by using all of their senses as appropriate
to find out about, and identify, some features of living things, objects and events they observe
to observe, find out about and identify features in the place they live and the natural world
to find out about their environment, and talk about those features they like and dislike

In Creative Development
to explore colour, texture, shape, form and space in two and three dimensions

Attracting insects to your garden

▶ **Don't use sprays** – or if you do, use insect friendly ones. (Look at page 45 for information on getting rid of pests safely).

▶ **Don't kill caterpillars** if you find them – or you won't get butterflies!

▶ **Leave a few untidy or wild places.** Very tidy gardens are not very insect friendly! Insects need places to lay their eggs, hatch their larvae or caterpillars and some need places to hibernate over the winter. Ivy provides good cover in winter for all sorts of insects. Boggy ground and shade are also favourite places for insect life.

▶ **Leave a log or two** and some dead leaves and grass in a corner as a hiding place for ladybirds, beetles and other bugs.

▶ **Grow old-fashioned varieties of flowers.** Some modern varieties don't produce nectar and pollen, vital for bees and butterflies.

▶ **Add a water feature** (see page 41). Water, even a small pool or fountain, will attract many insects, including dragonflies.

▶ **Plant some of the following flowers and bushes.** This is a reliable way to attract insects.

Aubretia – low growing, blue/purple flowers in May/June.

Sweet rocket – scented, white/violet/purple flowers in May – August.

Red valerian – often grows wild, likes dry soil, red flowers in summer.

Lavender – scented, blue/white/pink/purple flowers in summer.

Teasel – tall spiny heads with small pink flowers in late summer. The heads can be dried for flower arranging.

Honesty – pink/lavender flowers in summer, with seed heads like little purses of money. Can be dried for inside arrangement.

Scabious – blue/pink flowers throughout summer.

Buddleia – the butterfly bush has long blue/purple flowers in summer.

Golden rod – a tall feathery plant with golden spires of flowers in autumn.

Butterflies, bees and other insects like brightly coloured flowers. If the flower smells good, insects will be there!

Planting in Shady Places

If your garden area is in shade, don't despair! There are plenty of things you can do and a wide variety of plants you can grow.

What they are learning by growing plants in different places:

In Personal, Social and Emotional Development
to be confident to try new activities

Problem Solving, Reasoning and Numeracy
to use everyday words to describe position

In Knowledge and Understanding of the World
to ask questions about why things happen and how things work
to observe, find out about and identify features in the place they live and the natural world
to find out about their environment, and talk about
those features they like and dislike

In Physical Development
to handle tools, objects and materials safely and with increasing control

In Creative Development
to explore colour, texture, shape, form and space in two and three dimensions

Ideas for brighter gardens

▶ Try painting walls and fences white or bright, light-reflecting colours.

▶ Mount unbreakable mirrors to reflect light into the shady area.

▶ Hang reflective things from strings or mount them on surfaces – try old CDs, strips of foil and foil containers.

▶ Make some bright sculptures from cement or clay, and press reflective objects into the surfaces.

▶ If you are gardening indoors, put your plants near a window, reflect light by using a mirror, shine a light on them, or choose plants that don't like bright light! Most indoor plants don't like direct sunlight, especially in summer.

Some plants for shady places

Garden plants

▶ Hostas have lovely foliage (but slugs and snails love them!).

▶ Ferns like damp shade: water them well or plant them near a pond.

▶ Solomon's seal has lovely arching stems with flowers like single white bluebells. Cut them to the ground in autumn.

▶ Violets – white, purple or blue – will carpet a whole area over time.

▶ Ivy – all varieties will grow in shade, but the variegated ones may eventually turn green all over!

▶ Woodland plants like primroses, celandines and bluebells all like shade, but don't dig them up from the countryside – it's illegal! Get plants from garden centres or from friends' gardens.

Indoor plants (most flowering house plants need a bright position. Foliage plants survive best in partial or full shade)

▶ Aspidistra

▶ Ficus (weeping fig)

▶ Begonia

▶ Ferns (east or north facing window)

▶ Helxine (baby's tears)

▶ Palms

Wet Ones (water and bog plants)

You don't need a pond to grow water plants – a wet spot or a boggy corner is perfect for some of these plants that like to have wet feet.

What they are learning by growing plants in different places:

In Personal, Social and Emotional Development
to be confident to try new activities

Problem Solving, Reasoning and Numeracy
to use everyday words to describe position

In Knowledge and Understanding of the World
to ask questions about why things happen and how things work
to observe, find out about and identify features in the place they live and the natural world to find out about their environment, and talk about those features they like and dislike

In Physical Development
to handle tools, objects and materials safely and with increasing control

In Creative Development
to explore colour, texture, shape, form and space in two and three dimensions

Making a bog garden

Partial shade is a good place for a bog garden – not too shady, but not in direct midday sun.

You can make a bog garden like this:

▶ Dig a shallow hole (let the children help). Put the earth in a pile.

▶ Line the hole with plastic sheeting or pond liner.

▶ Put the soil back in the hole on top of the liner and tap it down.

▶ Cover the soil with a layer of gravel to keep it damp.

▶ Water the bog garden so it is very boggy and wet. You will need to maintain this state of wetness!

▶ Plant some bog plants (these are usually called marginal plants) such as : marsh marigold, any variety of iris, arum lilies, lady's mantle, astilbe, dicentra, geums, hostas, rushes, grasses, primulas, violas and violets.

▶ Make sure you keep your bog garden wet.

Making a safe pond

What you need:

▶ a container such as a big bucket, a shallow bath, a half barrel, a big patio pot with no hole in the bottom

▶ rain water (collect this in bowls or buckets)

▶ gravel, small stones and a couple of bricks

▶ some soil and some pond planting baskets

▶ some water plants such as duckweed, water soldiers, a small water lily and some marginals (see above).

What you do:

1. Test the container to make sure it is watertight. If it isn't, seal any leaks or holes with waterproof sealant (from a DIY shop).

2. Put the pond in a shady place.

3. Put some gravel and stones in the bottom of your pond.

4. Fill your pond with rain water.

5. Plant marginals in your pond baskets and float pond plants on the surface. A water lily will need its own pot and will need to be weighed down with a stone inside so it stays on the bottom of the pond.

    You could add a goldfish!

> **...and the cheap option!**
> Make bog and water gardens in old bowls, pans and trays. You don't need to make room for drainage.

Bulbs and Corms

Growing bulbs is a popular activity with children, both indoors and outdoors. They just need a bit of patience, but the surprise and the colour are worth waiting for!

What they are learning by growing bulbs:

In Personal, Social and Emotional Development
to continue to be interested and motivated

In Communication, Language and Literacy
to interact with others, negotiating plans and activities

Problem Solving, Reasoning and Numeracy
to extend their vocabulary

In knowledge of the world
to find out about, and identify, some features of living things
to look closely at change
to observe, find about out and identify features in the natural world

In Physical Development
to handle tools, objects and materials safely and with increasing control

In Creative Development
to respond in a variety of ways to what they see, hear, smell, touch and feel

Growing bulbs indoors

Try growing bulbs in water: You need small bulbs (crocus, grape hyacinth or narcissus); a shallow bowl; and gravel, small stones or glass beads. Put the stones etc. into the bowl and tuck the bulbs among them so just their points are above the surface. Add some water. Put them in a light place and they will begin to grow! Don't let them dry out, and give taller plants some support as they grow.

Plant some bulbs to flower for Christmas. You need prepared bulbs (ask at the garden centre) e.g. daffodils, hyacinths and crocuses. Plant them in September in compost in shallow bowls (the bulbs mustn't touch or the pot or they may rot). Leave just the tips showing. Put the bowls in a cool, dark place (your toy shed, the cellar or outside in a black bag). Leave them for 6 – 10 weeks, checking the soil is moist. Take out on 1st December and put in a warm, light place. Water and feed them and they should flower for Christmas.

Try growing a stunning amaryllis (you can almost watch them grow!) or a hyacinth in a bulb glass (where you can see the roots growing).

Growing bulbs outdoors

You could plant some bulbs in tubs or pots, window boxes or hanging baskets. You could plant some in the grass or beds in the garden, or you could do some community work and plant some for elderly neighbours, parents, friends or even the local shopping centre!

What you need:

▶ outdoor bulbs of any sort (daffodils, crocuses, narcissuses, tulips, snow drops etc.)

▶ compost for containers

▶ trowels or bulb planters (from a garden centre)

What you do:

1. Always plant bulbs at twice their own depth. Big bulbs need to be deeper or they fall over! Small bulbs need to be nearer the light.

2. To get a natural planting, toss handfuls of bulbs on the planting place and plant them where they fall. Otherwise they look a bit regimented.

3. Plant spring bulbs in the autumn.

4. Plant tubs with several sorts of bulbs (small varieties at the top) so you can enjoy them over a longer time.

...and the cheap option!
Wait until the end of the autumn and you may be able to get your bulbs cheaper!

Grow Bags

Grow bags are a cheap and effective way of growing plants and vegetables. You can use them in any place, indoors as well as outside. They are especially good for annuals and climbers – and of course for tomatoes.

What they are learning when they grow their own food:

In Personal, Social and Emotional Development
to continue to be interested, excited and motivated to learn

In Communication, Language and Literacy
to interact with others, negotiating plans

In Knowledge and Understanding of the World
to investigate objects and materials by using all of their senses as appropriate
to find out about, and identify, some features of living things and events they observe
to ask questions about why things happen to observe features in the natural world

In Physical Development
to recognise the importance of keeping healthy and those things which contribute to this

In Creative Development
to respond in a variety of ways to what they see, hear, smell, touch, taste and feel

What you need

▶ a grow bag (you can get several different sizes). Some are even small enough for window-sills.

▶ some tomato plants – two or three for each bag. (Child friendly varieties can be found on on page 58.)

▶ tomato food (liquid to mix with water)

▶ canes and string (or strips of old fabric)

▶ a hand sprayer (in case of bugs!)

> **...and the cheap option!**
> Put a notice up on the board asking parents and friends for tomato plants.
> They may have spare ones to give away!

What you do

1. Choose a sunny spot (inside or out) and put your grow bag close to a warm wall.
2. Plant your tomatoes in late spring once frosts have gone.
3. The grow bag will probably have instructions for use. If not, cut a cross in the plastic for each plant, fold the plastic back and put a plant in each little square hole you have made.
4. Push a cane in the compost near each plant, so you can support it as it grows. As the plants get bigger, tie them gently to the cane. You may need to tie the side shoots too, especially as the fruit starts to grow.
5. Water your tomatoes regularly and feed them once a week according to the instructions on the food container.
6. If you use bush or tumbling varieties, they don't need canes, but they may be more inviting to slugs and snails!

Pests!

Slugs, snails and whitefly love tomatoes! Hunt every day for slugs and snails, and remove them. There is a child-friendly spray to deter whitefly and greenfly. Or grow basil with tomatoes to deter bugs and add flavour to your salads!

> **Bug Buster!**
> Mix 3 tablespoons of washing up liquid with 1/3 of a cup of vegetable oil. Mix well and store in a safe place. Use two spoonfuls in your hand sprayer, top up with water and – spray away those bugs!

Other plants for grow bags

Try beans, marrows, melons or courgettes. Remember these plants are hungry and thirsty, and need regular drink and meals. Flowers like grow bags too. Try Sweet Peas, Nasturtiums and Morning Glory. Have you ever thought of putting a grow bag of flowers on your shed or porch roof?

Climb, Creep and Clamber

Climbers and creepers can brighten up the most unattractive areas. Choose from evergreens, annuals or perennials, with or without flowers. They can be used to cover an unsightly shed or fence, to make a screen between activities or as a focal point for your garden.

What they are learning by growing creepers and climbers:

In Personal, Social and Emotional Development
to be confident to try new activities

Problem Solving, Reasoning and Numeracy
to use everyday words to describe position

In Knowledge and Understanding of the World
to ask questions about why things happen and how things work
to observe, find out about and identify features in the place they live and the natural world
to find out about their environment, and talk about those features they like and dislike

In Physical Development
to handle tools, objects and materials safely and with increasing control

In Creative Development
to explore colour, texture, shape, form and space in two and three dimensions

Perennial climbers

- ivy
- mile a minute (Russian vine)
- jasmine
- solanus (potato plant)
- honeysuckle
- rosa lutea (a thornless rose)
- ornamental hop
- clematis

Or try living willow (see page 60)

Annual climbers

- sweet peas
- nasturtiums
- canary creeper
- morning glory
- Chilean glory vine
- runner beans

Making a screen of climbers

What you need:

- a piece of garden trellis
- a plastic or wooden plant trough
- two broom handles or pieces of timber (approx. 7x7cm and 1.25m long)
- hammer and nails, or screws and a screwdriver
- if you can't sink the uprights into the ground, you need two buckets and a bag of ready-mix concrete
- one or two climbing plants or some seeds; compost

...and the cheap option!
Use garden netting and string to make a screen that will give you fun for one summer.

What you do:

1. If you need to make your own supports, mix the concrete and fill the buckets half full. Put the posts in the concrete and leave to dry.

2. If you have soil, hammer the uprights into the ground (measure the trellis so you get them in the right place!)

3. Nail (or screw) the trellis to the uprights, leaving a space between the ground and the bottom of the trellis to fit your trough.

4. Put the trough at the bottom of the trellis.

5. Fill it with compost and plant your climbers.

6. Don't forget to water your plants and gently tie them to the trellis as they grow (especially if they don't have tendrils).

N.B. You could make an indoor living screen with ivy, jasmine or any climbing house plant.

A Gar-Den!

Dens and hideouts are always popular with children. Use some climbers or flowers to make a living den in your garden.

What they are learning when they make growing dens and houses:

In Personal, Social and Emotional Development
to continue to be interested, excited and motivated to learn and to be confident to try new activities

In Communication, Language and Literacy
to interact with others, negotiating plans and activities
to use talk to organise, sequence and clarify thinking, ideas, feelings and events

In Knowledge and Understanding of the World
to investigate objects and materials

by using all of their senses as appropriate
to find out about their environment, and talk about those features they like and dislike

Problem Solving, Reasoning and Numeracy
to use everyday words to describe position

In Physical Development
to move with control and co-ordination

What you need

▶ six or eight long canes (at least two metres each)
▶ runner bean seeds (or sweet peas for a scented den, or sunflowers)
▶ grass seed to make a green carpet
▶ string and some strips of fabric
▶ scissors and a trowel

What you do

1. Find a good, sunny spot in your garden (it's best on grass or soil). If you haven't got any soil, put the plants and the poles in buckets of compost or big plant pots with a heavy stone or brick in the bottom of each to make sure they are steady.

2. Draw a big letter C on the grass or ground (with paint, chalk or water). The opening in the C is for the door.

3. Dig six (or eight) holes equally spaced around the C and push a cane firmly into each one. Slope the canes towards the middle of the C.

4. Tie the canes near the top with some fabric strips (leave the ends loose to scare the birds away from your beans). If you choose bright colours they will also blow in the wind and look like flags!

5. Wind string loosely up each cane in a spiral (to help the beans or sweet peas to climb up). If you plant sunflowers, you will have to tie them to the canes as they grow.

6. In April, plant three bean seeds, sunflower seeds or sweet pea plants round each cane, and water well.

7. Wait and watch for the seeds to sprout, and gently encourage them to curl round the canes.

8. Water the plants regularly.

   Soon you will have a bean den or tepee, a scented flower bower, or a sunflower house just big enough for two children to play in. The bean den will have red flowers, lovely leaves and beans to eat!

   ▶ If you plant sunflowers, explain to the children that the flowers are very colourful but the leaves are a bit scratchy!

   ▶ You can make more permanent shelters with living willow (this only really works if you can plant it into the ground). The willow twigs take root and make a growing shelter which lasts all year round, growing bigger every year (see page 60).

Under the Ground

Some children find planting very frustrating, and want to dig seeds up to see how they are doing under the ground! Make sure you plant plenty of seeds or tubers to allow for investigations by these young gardeners!

What they are learning when they dig up plants and roots:

In Personal, Social and Emotional Development
to be confident to try new activities

Problem Solving, Reasoning and Numeracy
to use everyday words to describe position

In Knowledge and Understanding of the World
to ask questions about why things happen and how things work
to observe, find out about and identify features in the place they live and the natural world
to find out about their environment, and talk about those features they like and dislike

In Physical Development
to handle tools, objects and materials safely and with increasing control

In Creative Development
to explore colour, texture, shape, form and space in two and three dimensions

What you need for a potato barrel

- ▶ a half barrel, a plastic dustbin or other large container – the bigger and deeper, the better!
- ▶ compost; seed potatoes and trowels
- ▶ some smaller plant pots or buckets for investigators

What you do

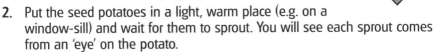

1. Seed potatoes have been specially prepared for sowing: look out for them in early spring.
2. Put the seed potatoes in a light, warm place (e.g. on a window-sill) and wait for them to sprout. You will see each sprout comes from an 'eye' on the potato.
3. When the shoots are about 20cm high, put a 10cm layer of compost in the bottom of your container and place the seed potatoes on top. Totally cover the potatoes and the shoots with compost.
4. Keep the compost moist.
5. Look at them every day and keep 'earthing them up' as they grow (this encourages the baby potatoes to form on underground stems, and stops them going green.
6. Keep earthing up until you reach the top of the container.
7. Now let the plants grow leaves (and their pretty white flowers).
8. If you chose an early variety, the potatoes will be ready to eat during the summer. If you chose a later variety, you will have to wait until September.
9. The best way to harvest your crop is to gently tip the container over until the plants tumble out. You will see the little potatoes among the compost, ready for you to pick up, cook and eat!

N.B. Harvesting with a fork is more difficult; the prongs may damage the potatoes.

Other good root crops to grow are carrots, radishes or beetroot (you can grow all of these in containers if you choose dwarf or miniature varieties – see page 58).

Meanwhile...

Plant some more potatoes in the 'experimental' pots or buckets. Let the children dig them up and plant them again as they grow. They will not be so successful after this experience, but they will give a lot of pleasure and interest. Remember, if the baby potatoes on these plants turn green, they should not be eaten!

Make Your Own Compost

Making your own compost is a fascinating yet simple operation. Weeds, leaves, peelings, apple cores and other vegetable waste are magically converted into crumbly compost to use in pots, tubs and containers.

What they are learning when they help make compost:

Problem Solving, Reasoning and Numeracy
to be confident to try new activities

In Communication, Language and Literacy
to interact with others, negotiating plans and activities
to extend their vocabulary, exploring the meanings and sounds of new words
to use talk to organise, sequence and clarify thinking, ideas, feelings and events

In Knowledge and Understanding of the World
to investigate objects and materials by using all of their senses as appropriate
to ask questions about why things happen and how things work
to find out about their environment, and talk about those features they like and dislike

You can make compost in any of these:

▶ a black plastic or fine mesh bag with holes in

▶ a small plastic or metal dustbin (or plastic laundry container)

▶ a circle of chicken wire on the ground

▶ a plastic barrel

▶ a ready-made compost bin

Notes:

a. All containers need holes in the sides so the compost can breathe. The bigger the container, the faster it will convert your compost! Smaller bins work – they just take longer.

b. Plastic containers will only really last a year.

c. Only vegetable matter should be composted – no meat, fish or cooked things. Sticks and hard wood will take longer to rot. Everything will rot more quickly if you chop or break it up.

What you do

1. Choose your container and put it somewhere in the shade. Protect it from too much rain with a plastic bag or sheet. A compost bin or heap should never dry out, but it shouldn't get too wet either!

2. Collect a layer of leaves, weeds or grass. Then add layers of other things – fruit peel and cores, salad leaves, weeds, grass clippings, egg shells, dead flowers, teabags etc.

3. Every week, sprinkle a thin layer of compost or soil over the things in the bin (this will help to deter flies) and keep the composter covered when you are not adding things.

4. Check daily to see if your compost needs a sprinkle of water.

5. When the container is full, cover it with a plastic sheet and leave for at least six months, when your compost should be ready. It should be dark and rich, like chocolate cake crumbs.

6. Use your compost in pots and containers or spread it on the garden (or sell it to raise money to buy plants and seeds!).

...and the cheap option
Fill black plastic bags with leaves in the autumn. Add some garden soil. Tie the tops of the bags and leave them behind your shed for two years. The leaves should turn into compost without you doing anything else!

Safe and Secure

Gardening and growing plants is a calming and rewarding activity for adults and children. However, we must make sure that children are safe when involved in any activity, and gardening is no exception.

What they are learning in a safe garden:

In Communication, Language and Literacy
to interact with others, negotiating plans and activities

In Knowledge and Understanding of the World
to investigate objects and materials by using all of their senses as appropriate
to observe, find out about and identify features in the place they live and the natural world

In Creative Development
to respond in a variety of ways to what they see, hear, smell, touch and feel

In Physical Development
to move with control and co-ordination
to recognise the importance of keeping healthy and those things which contribute to this
to use a range of small and large equipment
to handle tools, objects and materials safely and with increasing control

Supervision

▶ As with most activities, children need to be supervised when using garden tools and equipment. Independent access to the activity and to the tools should be planned and organised. Tools can be kept in baskets or on hooks in the shed. Gloves and other protective clothing can also be provided where children can help themselves while an adult keeps an eye on the proceedings.

▶ Children should also be reminded of safety aspects such as washing their hands after gardening, and avoiding putting objects (or dirty fingers) in their mouths.

▶ Some children may find working with soil distasteful to start with, and some will have allergies. You could offer these children gardening gloves to wear, so everyone can join in.

▶ You may find that a parent, elderly neighbour or friend of the school would enjoy working alongside the children in their gardening activities. Make sure they understand the rules too.

▶ Children should also be taught to handle plants, bugs and any small creatures they find with care and respect.

Tools and equipment

▶ Real, small-sized metal and wood tools are much more rewarding for children to use. Plastic or toy tools are frustrating and can be dangerous if they are used for real gardening. Tools should always be cleaned after use and stored where children can fetch them and put them away.

▶ Suitable tools for young children include trowels, hand forks, child sized spades and brooms. Add dibbers, hoes, rakes etc. for more ambitious projects.

▶ Indoor gardeners need equipment too. Miniature hand forks etc. are now available for indoor gardening. Try a garden centre for these.

▶ Add plastic pots, seeds, garden sticks, string, hand sprays, bug pots, magnifying glasses, plant labels, seed catalogues, books, and clip and white boards.

▶ Children should be taught the names and uses of the tools. They also need to be shown how to use them correctly.

Suppliers

▶ The best range of children's tools (spades, rakes, trowels, barrows etc. and children's gardening gloves) that we have found is the Brio range (see www.brio.co.uk for stockists, prices and catalogues).

...and the cheap option!
For most digging and gardening, children can manage with old metal spoons and forks.

Come and Help!

Gardening is a co-operative activity and there are many ways of getting other people involved in your projects.

What they are learning when they garden with others:

In Personal, Social and Emotional Development

to continue to be interested, excited and motivated to learn

In Communication, Language and Literacy

to interact with others, negotiating plans and activities

to extend their vocabulary, exploring the meanings and sounds of new words

In Knowledge and Understanding of the World

to ask questions about why things happen and how things work

to observe, find out about and identify features in the place they live and the natural world

to find out about their environment, and talk about those features they like and dislike

Parents

Many of the parents in your setting will be interested in gardening, indoors or out. Put a notice on your parents' notice board to invite them to donate plants, pots, cuttings, seeds and of course, time to help the children with their gardening activities. Some parents would also love to be involved in big digging, planting or building projects.

Community groups

Contact local gardening clubs and allotment groups. Recruit volunteers from youth groups, children's clubs and after school care. Have joint projects, go and visit local gardens, enter local shows, display your successes and put photos in free newspapers.

Garden centres

Garden centres and DIY stores are often very supportive of children's gardening – after all, they are developing future gardeners! You can get out of date seeds, plants that are past their best, sale items of tools and equipment and grow bags at special prices. And they deliver!

Friends

Try involving local neighbours and friends of the school – people living nearby, grandparents, big brothers and sisters, and local groups. Don't forget the friends and families of staff members who may be willing to contribute plants etc. Don't forget that seeds, cuttings, fruit stones and pips are free and everyone needs to keep looking!

Local shops

Local shops will often donate things to children, specially if they go and ask (with you) and send a thank you picture! Boxes, containers, string, envelopes, left-over plants and flowers are all possibilities. You could also offer to make tubs and hanging baskets for them (for the cost of the ingredients) or display photos of your projects or children's pictures.

The Internet

Look on the Internet for ideas and resources.
Try www.bbc.co.uk/gardening or www.123child.com

If you enter 'children' and 'gardening' in a search engine, such as Google or Lycos, you will get lots of gardening ideas. Or try American sites for children and teachers.

Fruit and Vegetable Varieties

The plants listed below are suitable for young children to grow with help from adults.

	Variety	Notes
Apple	Choose M27 types for small trees	
Blackberry	Merton Thornless	Not too vigorous
	Oregon Thornless	
Bean	Blue Lake French	Climbing
	Scarlet Emperor	Runner, red flowers
	Gulliver Dwarf	Runner
Blueberry	Bluecrop	Good autumn leaves
	Jersey	Vigorous, big berries
Carrot	Nantes	Fast growing, good flavour
Courgette	Defender	Disease-resistant
Cress	Fine Curled	Good all year round
Gooseberry	Leveller	Good flavour, dessert
	Warrington	Good for eating and jam
Lamb's lettuce	Jade	
Melon	Minnesota Midget	Small, fast growing
Pea	Oregon Sugar Pod	Mangetout, very sweet
	Feltham First	Early, very hardy
Potato	Charlotte	Good hot or cold
Pumpkin	Sunny F1	Good flavour
	Mammoth	Giant size!
Rhubarb	Glaskin's Perpetual	Reliable and productive
Salad		
Lettuce	Salad Bowl	Cut and come again
	Tom Thumb	Small, quick growing
Strawberry	Belle de Meaux	Alpine, crimson
	Baron Solemacher	Alpine, taller
Tayberry	Medana	
Tomato	Plum Inca's F1	Bush plant, no staking
	Gardener's Delight	Cherry, heavy cropper
	Tumbler	Cascading good cropper

Flowers You CAN eat!

Safety warning! Eating flowers is fun, but should always be done under strict supervision. Make sure that the flowers you eat have been grown by you (or someone you know). Don't eat flowers from florists or those you see near roads – they may have been contaminated by harmful chemicals.

	Petals of flower head	Whole flower	Eat seeds or berries	Use leaves as well	Make sorbet	Make jam or jelly	Add to soup	Infuse in oil	Good in salads	Make herb butter	Crystalise	Add to honey
Sweet violets		●			●	●			●		●	
Nasturtiums		●							●			
Pot marigolds	●		●				●		●			
Carnations and pinks	●							●	●		●	
Daisies	●						●					
Elderflowers and berries		●	●			●						
Roses	●				●	●					●	●
Sunflowers	●		●						●			
Basil		●		●			●		●	●		
Chives		●		●			●		●	●		
Rocket		●		●			●		●	●		
Lavender		●						●				●
Beans and peas		●							●			
Thyme		●		●				●	●			●

To crystalise violets, pinks or rose petals: pick the flowers when they have just come out; don't wait until they are past their best! Whisk up some fresh or powdered egg white. Dip the flowers or rose petals in the whisked egg white, then dip them gently in caster sugar. Leave them to dry on greaseproof paper in a warm place or a very very low oven (not the microwave!). Use to decorate cakes or biscuits.

And Finally...

Why not plant some living willow in your garden? You can make it into shelters, bowers, tunnels, seats, screens and dividers.

All you need to do is:

▶ order the twigs, so you can plant them between January and April

▶ push the twigs into the ground

▶ keep them well watered and they will grow!

Willow likes to be wet, so make sure you put them somewhere easy to water or where their roots will be damp and cool. When they start to grow, trim them if they get unruly, and bend and tie them into the shape you want.

Get living willow from:

P H Coates and Son
Meare Green Court
Stoke St Gregory
Taunton
Somerset
TA3 6HY
Tel: 01823 490249
www.coates-willowbaskets.co.uk

At the time of writing, the BBC website has a special feature on living willow (www.bbc.co.uk/gardening). By the time you read this, it might not still be there, but it's always worth looking at the BBC gardening website, which is a consistently reliable source of ideas and inspiration.

If you have found this book useful you might also like ...

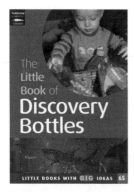

LB Discovery Bottles
ISBN 978-1-9060-2971-5

LB Christmas
ISBN 978-1-9022-3364-2

LB Making Poetry
ISBN 978-1-4081-1250-2

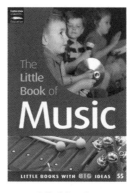

LB Music
ISBN 978-1-9041-8754-7

All available from
www.acblack.com/featherstone/

More titles in the Little Books series include ...

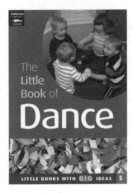

LB Dance
ISBN 978-1-9041-8774-5

LB Bags, Boxes and Trays
ISBN 978-1-9050-1909-0

LB Clothes and Fabrics
ISBN 978-1-9050-1969-4

LB Sound Ideas
ISBN 978-1-9050-1955-7

All available from
www.acblack.com/featherstone/

The Little Books Club

There is always something in Little Books to help and inspire you.
Packed full of lovely ideas, Little Books meet the need for exciting and
practical activities that are fun to do, address the Early Learning Goals
and can be followed in most settings. Everyone is a winner!

We publish 5 new Little Books a year. Little Books Club members receive
each of these 5 books as soon as they are published for a reduced price.
The subscription cost is £37.50 – a one off payment that buys
the 5 new books for £7.50 instead of £8.99 each.

In addition to this, Little Books Club Members receive:
· Free postage and packing on anything ordered from the
  Featherstone catalogue
· A 15% discount voucher upon joining which can be used to buy any
  number of books from the Featherstone catalogue
· Members price of £7.50 on any additional Little Book purchased
· A regular, free newsletter dealing with club news, special offers and
  aspects of Early Years curriculum and practice
· All new Little Books on approval - return in good condition within 30
  days and we'll refund the cost to your club account

Call 020 7440 2446 or email: littlebooks@acblack.com for
an enrolment pack. Or download an application form from our website:
www.acblack.com/featherstone

The **Little Books** series consists of:

All Through the Year
Bags, Boxes & Trays
Bricks and Boxes
Celebrations
Christmas
Circle Time
Clay and Malleable Materials
Clothes and Fabrics
Colour, Shape and Number
Cooking from Stories
Cooking Together
Counting
Dance
Dance, with music CD
Discovery Bottles
Dough
50
Fine Motor Skills
Fun on a Shoestring
Games with Sounds
Growing Things
ICT
Investigations
Junk Music
Language Fun
Light and Shadow

Listening
Living Things
Look and Listen
Making Books and Cards
Making Poetry
Mark Making
Maths Activities
Maths from Stories
Maths Songs and Games
Messy Play
Music
Nursery Rhymes
Outdoor Play
Outside in All Weathers
Parachute Play
Persona Dolls
Phonics
Playground Games
Prop Boxes for Role Play
Props for Writing
Puppet Making
Puppets in Stories
Resistant Materials
Role Play
Sand and Water
Science through Art
Scissor Skills

Sewing and Weaving
Small World Play
Sound Ideas
Storyboards
Storytelling
Seasons
Time and Money
Time and Place
Treasure Baskets
Treasureboxes
Tuff Spot Activities
Washing Lines
Writing

All available from

www.acblack.com/featherstone